AGATHA
CHRISTIE

Agatha Christie

Writer of Mystery

Carol Dommermuth-Costa

LERNER PUBLICATIONS COMPANY · MINNEAPOLIS

To Chris,
my twin soul

Illustrations by John Erste
Text & illustrations copyright © 1997 by Lerner Publications Company

Library of Congress Cataloging-in-Publication Data

Dommermuth-Costa, Carol.
    Agatha Christie : writer of mystery / Carol Dommermuth-Costa.
      p.   cm.
    Includes bibliographical references and index.
    Summary: A biography of the English mystery writer who, after creating Hercule Poirot and Miss Marple, became a Dame Commander of the British Empire.
    ISBN 0-8225-4954-9 (alk. paper)
      1. Christie, Agatha, 1890–1976—Biography—Juvenile literature.
    2. Women authors, English—20th century—Biography—Juvenile literature. 3. Detective and mystery stories—Authorship—Juvenile literature. [1. Christie, Agatha, 1890–1976. 2. Authors, English. 3. Women—Biography.]   I. Title.
    PR6005.H66Z597 1997
    823'.912—dc20   96–34435

Manufactured in the United States of America
1 2 3 4 5 6 – JR – 02 01 00 99 98 97

Contents

From a very young age, Agatha loved to read. Often she would steal away to read under her favorite shrub.

⚜ ONE ⚜

Ashfield

1890–1899

Six-year-old Agatha Miller snuggled deeper into her pillows and pulled the down coverlet up to her chin. She waited patiently for her mother to begin her bedtime story.

Mrs. Miller was a wonderful storyteller. Perhaps her stories were not quite proper for a young child, but Agatha loved them. She told Agatha tales of poisoned candles, of a world found beneath a stream, of vampire's blood and deserted hotels.

These stories did not frighten Agatha. Instead, they aroused her intense curiosity about the unknown. This interest in mystery would remain with Agatha for the rest of her life.

Agatha Mary Clarissa Miller was born on September 15, 1890. She and her family lived in the town of Torquay on the southern coast of England.

Agatha believed that "one of the luckiest things that can happen to you in life, is, I think, to have a happy childhood. I had a very happy childhood." Agatha's world was filled with caring adults, parents who didn't argue, loyal servants, grandmothers who doted on her every whim, and warm celebrations for the special occasions in her life. She was allowed to do almost anything she wanted—as long as she was having fun.

Agatha's parents, Clara and Frederick Miller, had a deep and loving relationship. Clara adored her husband, whom she had known since childhood. Frederick thought that Clara was "the finest wife a man could be blessed with."

*Frederick Miller,
Agatha's father*

Clara Miller,
Agatha's mother

Agatha described her father as "a very agreeable man." Mr. Miller made friends easily and people enjoyed his company. Mr. Miller had inherited enough money to support his family comfortably, and he didn't have to work for a living. Each morning he could be seen leaving the house after breakfast to take a leisurely stroll to the country club in Torquay. He often stopped at the local art gallery on the way. At lunchtime, Mr. Miller would return home for his meal and then return to the club to play croquet with some friends.

Mrs. Miller was very different from her husband. She was shy and sometimes lacked self-confidence. Yet she was an independent woman, highly creative, and open to new ideas. She firmly believed that her children could do anything they set their minds to. Mrs. Miller especially reinforced this belief in Agatha and Madge, Agatha's older sister. This was unusual at a time when most women were taught that there were limits to their career choices.

Like Agatha, Mrs. Miller loved mysteries and was curious about the unknown. She became involved in several religions, searching for answers to the mysteries of life and death. Agatha's mother also wrote poetry and short stories, often exploring the occult in her writing. One of the stories she wrote, "Mrs. Jordan's Ghost," told of sad but dead Mrs. Jordan, who appeared every time a particular piece of music was played on the piano.

There was another side to Agatha's mother. Agatha once wrote that her mother had "curious flashes of intuition—of knowing suddenly what other people were thinking." When Mrs. Miller was in the room, Agatha and her sister were careful not to even *think* about anything they didn't want her to know.

The Millers lived in a large, beautiful house called Ashfield—named for the abundance of ash trees on the grounds. Ashfield had an interesting design. Half of the house was two stories high, the other part three stories. Stained-glass windows decorated many rooms on the lower floor. French doors opened into the garden.

Art and collectibles cluttered every one of the house's large rooms. Agatha's father had made collecting his hobby, and he couldn't resist stopping at the galleries in Torquay on his daily walks, to purchase whatever drew his attention. He filled almost every available space with vases, figurines, statues, and knickknacks.

Agatha's favorite part of Ashfield was the gardens, or

grounds. She saw the grounds in three distinct parts: the kitchen garden, the main garden, and the woods. In the kitchen garden, the family grew vegetables and fruit trees, with plenty of Agatha's favorite raspberries and green apples. The main garden was the sprawling lawn at the front and sides of the house, generously decorated with potted plants and a large variety of trees. Each of the Miller children had adopted a special tree for sitting in and climbing during their outdoor playtime.

The third part of the garden was behind the house. A path led through the woods to a tennis court and a croquet lawn. To Agatha, the silence of the woods seemed to hold many secrets. Sunlight filtered ever so slightly through the tall trees. Leaving the path and strolling through these woods, Agatha felt that she had come upon a magical place.

Sometimes Agatha felt lonely at Ashfield. She had a brother and a sister, but she often felt like an only child. Madge, eleven years older than Agatha, was away at school during most of Agatha's girlhood. When Madge did come home on visits, she and Agatha shared many good times. Madge, like her mother, told wonderful stories, and Agatha loved to listen. Madge also played practical jokes on Agatha and scared her younger sister a number of times with her disguises. But Agatha liked being scared, and she encouraged Madge's games.

Monty, Agatha's brother, was ten years older than Agatha. She saw even less of Monty than she did of Madge. Monty was also away at school for most of Agatha's childhood. After he graduated, he joined the Royal Air Force and then settled in India.

Agatha was influenced by several memorable women in her childhood. In addition to her mother and Madge, Agatha had two grandmothers. Auntie-Grannie was Mr. Miller's stepmother, and Grannie Boehmer was Clara's mother. Auntie-Grannie had a huge house in a town called Ealing, where she lived by herself with several servants. This house was the meeting place for the two grandmothers, who spent afternoons reminiscing about their childhood while they laughed and teased each other.

Agatha enjoyed visiting Ealing. Large, sturdy mahogany furniture and hundreds of books filled the rooms. Agatha spent hours playing with imaginary companions in Auntie-Grannie's vast garden.

Frederick Miller's stepmother, known to all as Auntie-Grannie, doted on Agatha.

Another woman in Agatha's life made a deep and lasting impression—her nurse, affectionately called Nursie. Nursie took care of Agatha until she was about six years old. Nursie would never tell how old she was, and it was great fun in the Miller household to try to guess.

Of all the rooms in the house, Agatha loved the nursery best. Mauve wallpaper depicted irises climbing up to the ceiling. Agatha's bed was tucked behind a screen so that while she slept, Nursie could sit in her rocking chair and sew by the light of a small lamp. Mrs. Miller would come to tuck Agatha into bed. If time allowed, her mother would tell her a story.

Agatha delighted in her mother's tales of mystery and adventure. No two stories were ever the same. Nursie, on the other hand, was not as inventive. She told Agatha the same three or four stories over and over again. But Agatha didn't mind a bit and usually requested a story from Nursie whenever they went for a walk.

By the time Agatha turned five, she wanted to learn to read. After someone read her a story, Agatha would pick up the book and pretend to read. On their walks, Agatha often questioned Nursie about words that she saw printed on signs. Then one day Agatha surprised Nursie by reading a book aloud to her. Nursie ran to tell Mrs. Miller that Agatha could read.

Instead of being happy about her daughter's new skill, Mrs. Miller was upset. She believed that it was unhealthy for a child to read before the age of eight. But she couldn't do anything about it by then. Agatha was on her way to becoming an avid reader. When she was asked what she wanted for her birthday or Christmas, Agatha had only one answer—books.

Like many girls in the 1890s, Agatha read and reread Louisa May Alcott's book *Little Women*. She also enjoyed the works of Frances Hodgson Burnett, especially *The Secret Garden* and *Granny's Wonderful Chair.*

Mrs. Miller tried to curtail Agatha's reading. Agatha was not allowed to read in the morning. Mrs. Miller decided that mornings should be reserved for activities such as sewing, studying, and playing the piano. Agatha tried to obey, but sometimes she just couldn't wait until the afternoon. So she would take her book and sneak off to a corner of the garden, hiding under the bushes.

Mrs. Miller also believed that Agatha did not need a formal education—she could receive a fine education at home, through Mr. Miller's tutelage and the wealth of books in Ashfield's library. Noticing his younger daughter's quick mind with numbers, Mr. Miller began by teaching Agatha arithmetic. He also taught her to write.

But Agatha had a deeper thirst for learning. She thoroughly explored the books in the Miller library, discovering encyclopedias, dictionaries, and atlases. Agatha spent hours absorbing facts about people and places in the world.

Agatha didn't have any friends who lived near Ashfield. Lacking playmates, she spent many hours creating ways to amuse herself. One of her favorite toys was a simple hoop. This toy gave her many hours of fun. In her imagination the hoop became a seahorse, a monster, or a means of transportation.

Agatha also had several imaginary playmates: Mrs. Benson and the Kittens, Dick and Dick's mistress, a kingdom of Kings and Queens, and a school of girls Agatha's age. Agatha also doted on her pets: a cat, a dog named Toby, and Goldie, the canary.

Agatha loved to sit and play in her special cart, which was sometimes pulled by a real goat.

Early in 1899, Mr. Miller decided to move the family to the European continent for a short while. His funds had dwindled over the years, and Ashfield's expenses had become more than he could afford. Many English families found it more economical to live for part of each year in Europe. The Millers were no exception. They rented out Ashfield and left for the South of France.

Agatha and her mother in Paris

TWO

Becoming an Adult

1900–1908

Life in France was exciting for nine-year-old Agatha. She now had playmates her own age. The Selwyn sisters, Mary and Dorothy, were the first friends Agatha made. The Selwyns lived at the same hotel as the Millers in Pau, France. The three girls became constant companions and had much fun together, especially when they were being mischievous.

One of Agatha's favorite activities was organizing races up and down the hotel's long halls. But the hotel's other residents finally complained about the raucous laughter and screaming outside their rooms, and the races had to be moved outdoors.

Another time, Agatha and her friends silently crept into the hotel's vacant dining room. Moving from table to table, they filled all the salt shakers with sugar. The unsuspecting guests sprinkled sugar on their food instead of salt, rendering their meals inedible. Children weren't allowed in the formal dining room, so Agatha and her friends could only imagine the effects of their practical joke. They burst into laughter every time they thought about what they had done.

This camaraderie was good for the usually shy Agatha. In September of 1900, however, the Millers decided to leave Pau and visit Paris. Agatha had to say good-bye to her friends.

After a short stay in Paris, the Millers prepared to return to Ashfield. Suddenly, Mr. Miller became very ill. Doctors told him that he was suffering from heart disease, and he would have to curtail his activities. Mr. Miller accepted this news with his usual optimistic attitude, but Agatha and her mother were shaken.

When the Millers arrived back home in England, Mr. Miller's illness seemed to overshadow everything. He consulted with many specialists, but no one was able to help him. In November 1901, after suffering more than thirty minor heart attacks, Agatha's father died.

Devastated, Mrs. Miller went into deep mourning. Eleven-year-old Agatha recognized that her happy and secure life with two loving parents was gone forever. "We were no longer the Millers—a family. We were now two people living together, a middle-aged woman and an untried, naïve girl," she recalled.

Her father's sudden passing made Agatha realize how swiftly death could take someone away. She became very anxious about her mother's health. Agatha's worst fear was that her mother would be run over by a tram or die in her sleep. For weeks after Agatha's father died, she crept into her mother's bedroom at night to listen for the sounds of her breathing. Finally she began to sleep on a cot in a corner of Mrs. Miller's bedroom so that she could be at hand if her mother became ill during the night.

Soon after her husband's death, Mrs. Miller told Agatha that she wanted to sell Ashfield. She was afraid that the money left from Mr. Miller's estate wouldn't be enough to cover the house's expenses. Agatha thought her heart was going to break a second time. She hastily wrote notes to Madge—who lived a few miles away—and to Monty in India. She asked them to help her persuade their mother to keep Ashfield.

Mrs. Miller saw how much her children, especially Agatha, loved Ashfield. She understood Agatha's feelings. Agatha had just lost her father. It would be difficult to leave her beloved home as well. Mrs. Miller promised to keep Ashfield for as long as she could afford it.

Agatha's mother also came to realize that she and Agatha needed a short break from all the painful memories Ashfield held. She decided to take Agatha to Paris for a few weeks.

Agatha adored the glamour of Paris.

Agatha enjoyed L'Avenue de l'Opera, or Avenue of the Opera.

Paris offered a relaxing, enjoyable diversion for Agatha. During the day, she and her mother visited museums and had lunch or tea at one of the many cafés that lined the streets. They watched artists set up their easels on the sidewalks to paint. In the evenings, Agatha and her mother attended plays or the opera, or dined out with friends.

When they returned to Ashfield, Agatha and her mother fell into a quiet, comfortable life. They shared the chores at Ashfield and took long walks through Torquay. They often spent their evenings reading novels and poetry aloud to each other. Agatha especially loved the poetry of Henry Wadsworth Longfellow and Emily Dickinson.

In 1902, Agatha published a short poem in the local newspaper. The inspiration for her poem was the new tram service scheduled to run through Torquay. This modern development upset many local residents. Agatha's poem outlined the situation:

> When first the electric trams did run
> In all their scarlet glory,
> 'Twas well, but ere the day was done,
> It was another story.

At the age of twelve, Agatha began classes at Miss Guyer's Girls' School in Torquay. Two days a week she studied algebra, grammar, and spelling. A year and a half later, Mrs. Miller decided to send Agatha to study in France. She thought that Agatha needed to broaden her experience of the world, and she worried that her daughter had become too dependent on her. Mademoiselle T., the schoolmistress in Paris, welcomed Agatha warmly. Madge had attended the same school years before.

At first, Agatha was intensely homesick. She lost her appetite. Every time she thought of her mother, tears filled her eyes. Then, after spending a day with her mother, the homesickness vanished. She returned to school with anticipation of all that it had to offer.

Agatha spent the next two years studying mathematics, history, geography, and French. Although she had no trouble speaking or understanding French, she often felt frustrated by her difficulty reading and writing the language.

Agatha made many friends at school. She also spent a lot of time with her mother's friends, who invited her to the opera and to art gallery openings in and around Paris. For the first time in her life she began to enjoy dressing up.

Agatha and her friends wore their fanciest clothes to Torquay's many garden parties.

Once while visiting, Mrs. Miller took Agatha to a dressmaker in Paris to have some clothes made for formal occasions. Agatha found it exciting to choose material, to stand on the dressmaker's stool while she was being measured, and then to watch that material become a beautiful dress.

Agatha also learned dancing and etiquette. She learned to sit properly, to move gracefully, and to curtsy. She was drilled in the proper ways to speak to young men.

The only class Agatha really hated was painting lessons. Twice a week, Agatha and another student took the bus to the flower market (young girls did not travel alone in Paris). There they received instruction in still-life painting. They painted violets, lilies, and daffodils. Agatha did not excel in painting, and she felt frustrated in her efforts to render the flowers on paper.

At fifteen, Agatha completed her schooling in France. When she returned to Ashfield, her social life changed.

Agatha was now old enough to make friends on her own, and she soon became acquainted with other young girls in Torquay. Mrs. Miller encouraged Agatha to socialize.

Torquay was filled with all kinds of activities and amusements. Tea parties and garden parties took place on the immense lawns of friends' homes. When invited to such parties, Agatha and her friends took care to appear in their most becoming outfits. Fashions included high-heeled patent leather shoes, long skirts, and muslin blouses with starched and boned collars that often left rashes on the girls' necks.

Roller skating up and down Torquay's pier was another popular pastime, as were carousel rides during the yearly fair. Sometimes Agatha and her friends watched the yachting races while dining on raw mussels, oysters, and soda pop.

Roller skating was another favorite pastime for Torquay's young people.

Agatha enjoyed her close friendships, but she also loved to be alone. She loved to swim, and the seaside was her first choice for a place to think and dream. Agatha thought nothing of walking two or three miles to spend time at her favorite beach.

The library at Ashfield contained more than fifty classics. By the time she turned fifteen, Agatha had read most of the works of Sir Walter Scott and William Makepeace Thackeray. She devoured all the works by her favorite author, Charles Dickens. She cried over the death of Dorrit in his novel *Little Dorrit,* and she loved the romance of *Great Expectations.* Agatha read *The Three Musketeers* and *The Count of Monte Cristo* by French author Alexandre Dumas. She also adored the science fiction tales of Jules Verne, the poetry of Lord Byron, and the novels of George Eliot, Charlotte and Emily Brontë, and Rudyard Kipling.

Despite her love of literature, Agatha never dreamed of becoming a writer. She wanted what most other teenage girls in her day wanted: to marry a nice young man and raise a family. But she did have a few other ambitions.

From an early age, Agatha took delight in music and theater. While at school in Paris, she studied both piano and opera. She continued her lessons after her return to Torquay. Soon, Agatha decided to become a concert pianist. She dreamed of becoming famous and being invited to play in concert halls all over Europe. Her ambition was extinguished, however, when she performed one day for a countess who was herself an excellent pianist. As Agatha sat down at the piano, she grew so anxious that she played badly, hitting many wrong notes. Afterward her teacher told her that he didn't think she had the right temperament to perform in public.

Novelist Charlotte Brontë (above) and poet Lord Byron were two of Agatha's best-liked writers.

Disappointed but not discouraged, Agatha chose to concentrate on voice lessons and become an opera singer. One day a family friend who sang with the Metropolitan Opera in New York City asked Agatha to sing for her. After attentively listening to Agatha perform several arias, the professional singer told Agatha that although she would make a fine concert singer, her voice was simply not strong enough for the opera.

Disheartened, Agatha decided to drop her singing lessons. But she remained philosophical about her situation.

She told herself, "If the thing you want beyond anything cannot be, it is much better to recognize it and go forward instead of dwelling on one's regrets and hopes."

When Agatha was about seventeen, a bad case of flu kept her in bed for several days. She read until her eyes hurt and played solitaire until she was thoroughly bored. Noticing her daughter's restlessness, Mrs. Miller suggested that Agatha try to write a story.

Agatha was rather taken aback. She told her mother that she didn't think she could. But Mrs. Miller challenged her, demanding to know why not. Agatha realized that she couldn't answer her mother's question. Mrs. Miller continued to encourage Agatha, insisting that she would never know what she might be capable of until she tried.

Agatha had some difficulty getting started. She couldn't think of anything to write about. She jotted down some ideas and a story began to unfold in her mind. But how would she go about writing it?

Agatha decided that a good writer is also a good storyteller, so she would just tell the story. Once Agatha started writing, she didn't want to stop. She had fun creating characters and moving them around in the story. She wrote for a couple days and then Mrs. Miller brought Madge's old typewriter down from the attic. Agatha typed up her story, titling it "House of Beauty." The story was imaginative and well constructed for an amateur writer. It included many mysterious elements: strange dreams, hints of madness, and a "strangely beautiful house."

Encouraged, Agatha wrote four more short stories. She wanted to send her stories out to magazines for possible publication. After all, Madge had published two or three stories. Why couldn't Agatha be as successful?

Agatha as a young woman

Agatha decided to write under a pseudonym, or false name. Using a pseudonym was common practice for women writers, who often experienced prejudice for trying to succeed in what was considered "a man's field." Madge had already published under a male name. Agatha chose the names Mack Miller and Nathaniel Miller (her grandfather's name). The names made little difference, however, because Agatha's stories received rejection notices. But these rejections only fired her determination. As soon as a story came back to her, she would mail it off to another publisher. Agatha promised herself that she wouldn't give up until she had published her stories.

Egypt's archaeological past fascinated Agatha.

❧ THREE ❧

New Beginnings

1909–1918

After Agatha had received several rejection notices, her mother came to the rescue once again. She suggested that Agatha send one of her short stories to a friend of the family, the well-known writer Eden Phillpotts. After reading Agatha's story "Snow upon the Desert," Mr. Phillpotts sent her a letter with suggestions for improvement.

He told her to make her dialogue more natural and to resist the temptation to preach to her readers. He instructed Agatha to let her characters speak for themselves. Mr. Phillpotts knew that any criticism should also be peppered with some praise. He told Agatha that she had a natural sense of how to construct a story. He encouraged her to continue writing and told her that he believed she would go far. Agatha was grateful for this reassurance and support. She vowed to keep on writing and improving her craft.

Agatha felt happy, believing that her future was unfolding before her as she put her pen to paper. Her mother could not share Agatha's enthusiasm, however. Clara had not been well for a long time. Her depression and heartache over the death of her husband began to show in several physical ailments. In 1910, after going from doctor to doctor with few results, Clara decided that the best medicine would be a change of scenery. She and Agatha would go to Egypt. Agatha received this news with excitement. She hoped that her experiences in Egypt might inspire future stories.

In 1910 a trip to Egypt was not expensive. Many English people chose this country as a vacation spot. Clara was certain that both she and Agatha would make plenty of new acquaintances. Clara also hoped that Agatha might meet an interesting young man in Egypt. She did not feel it was too early for Agatha to begin thinking of marriage.

Agatha found much to keep her busy in romantic Cairo.

When Agatha and her mother arrived in Cairo, Egypt, they stayed at the Gezirah Palace Hotel. They attended polo matches, horse races, picnics, and dances. Agatha loved to dance and she was a fine dancer. She had trouble, however, in the art of conversation.

Agatha was shy and had difficulty starting or carrying on conversations with the men who asked her to dance. Many of them thought her quiet manner meant that she didn't like them, so they did not ask her to dance a second time. But enough young men attended these events that Agatha didn't have to worry about sitting out many dances. In fact, Cairo's busy social calendar kept Agatha quite busy, leaving her little time for writing. She even declined sightseeing tours and trips to the museums with her mother in order to be with her new friends.

After returning home from Egypt, Agatha joined social activities in and around Torquay. She became romantically involved with Bolton Fletcher, a young colonel in the British military. After seeing Agatha only twice, Bolton showered her with ardent love letters, flowers, books, and other gifts. On his third visit to Ashfield, he proposed marriage. Agatha felt flattered by the attention, but she didn't love Bolton. She turned down his proposal. Six months later Agatha received another marriage proposal from the persistent young man, this time by way of a telegram. She again declined.

A few months later, Agatha met Wilfred Pirie, a lieutenant in the navy. Their time together led to a friendship. Agatha also became attached to his family. She admired Mrs. Pirie, who was lively, confident, well read, and creative. When Wilfred asked Agatha to marry him, she found herself thinking of the practical, rather than romantic, possibilities of this marriage. For instance, Agatha knew that if she married Wilfred she would still be close enough to Torquay to spend time with her mother at Ashfield. A few months later, Wilfred wrote to Agatha asking if she would mind if he took a trip to South Africa on his leave instead of coming home to see her. She realized that she didn't care whether he came home or not. Realizing her feelings for Wilfred were more like those between a sister and brother than a wife and husband, she ended the relationship.

On October 12, 1912, when Agatha was twenty-two years old, she attended a party given by a Lord and Lady Chudleigh. She met a young man there named Archie Christie. Agatha learned that Archie had graduated from the Woolwich Military Academy, a prestigious school for military training.

Archie and Agatha danced together several times that night, but made no arrangements to see each other again. About ten days later, Agatha was visiting at a friend's house when she received a phone call from her mother. Mrs. Miller told Agatha that a young man was waiting for her and that she should come home immediately because he was determined not to leave without seeing her. When Agatha arrived home, she found Archie Christie waiting. He greeted Agatha and hesitantly asked if she remembered him from the dance.

After that, Archie and Agatha spent many days together, riding his motorbike through the countryside, dining at Ashfield with Mrs. Miller, or enjoying themselves at concerts and dances. Archie told Agatha about his career goals. Aviation was his passion. He had applied to the Royal Flying Corps and was waiting to hear about his acceptance. In January 1913—just three months after meeting Agatha— Archie was accepted into the Corps. He told Agatha that he was being relocated to another part of England, and asked her to marry him. She hesitated for one long moment. She knew that she and Archie often differed in their likes, dislikes, opinions, and beliefs. But the differences seemed to make Archie more attractive to her. Agatha said yes and excitedly rushed home to tell her mother.

Clara was not happy about the news. She liked Archie and thought that he was a fine friend for Agatha. She had hoped, however, that Agatha would marry a man with enough money to help with the upkeep of Ashfield.

Clara asked Agatha to wait a while before rushing into marriage. She pointed out that Archie would not be able to support Agatha on his meager salary. Clara hoped that the delay would allow Agatha to meet someone more financially stable.

Agatha met Archibald Christie at a party.

Archie flew with the British Royal Flying Corps during World War I.

Archie was more upset than Agatha was about the wait. The separation was difficult for both of them, and they almost broke up several times during the eighteen months apart. Agatha was beside herself with worry because Archie had told her that he wanted to volunteer for only the most dangerous assignments. Agatha was also busy caring for her mother. Clara had developed cataracts and there was a chance that she would soon be completely blind. Agatha almost broke off her engagement, anticipating that Clara would need her in the future.

In August 1914, with the assassination of Archduke Franz Ferdinand of Serbia, the long-unstable situation in Europe erupted into war. Germany declared war on Russia and France, and England declared war on Germany. World War I had begun. Archie's Royal Flying Corps was one of the first military divisions to be sent into battle. Archie sent Agatha a telegram asking to see her before he left England for the battlefields of France.

Agatha and Clara boarded a train to Southampton, a city on the southern coast of England. Because of several delays along the way, by the time they arrived, Agatha and Archie had only a few hours together. They didn't know if they would ever see each other again.

When Agatha returned home, she decided to help with the war effort by volunteering at the local hospital. Although she had some knowledge of first aid, Agatha was not qualified to be a nurse. As a nurse's aide, Agatha did all the chores that the nurses did not have time for. She cleaned floors, emptied bedpans, and disinfected medical supplies. She also helped in the operating room and visited with patients.

This demanding and tiring job left Agatha with little time to worry about Archie. For almost a year, they kept in

Agatha and Clara visited Archie in Southampton before he left for France.

touch through letters. Then Archie finally got a few weeks' leave. He immediately sent Agatha a telegram asking her to meet him in London.

This time it was Agatha who tried to pressure Archie into getting married. She feared that the many separations would destroy their relationship. But Archie declined. It just wasn't practical, he said. He could be killed and then she would be left a widow—possibly with a child to raise. A week later, however, Archie changed his mind. Perhaps he had fears similar to Agatha's. The two agreed to get married before Archie completed his leave.

Agatha and Archie married on Christmas Eve in 1915. Arranging a wedding on such short notice wasn't easy. But the young couple managed to obtain the required marriage license, engage a minister to perform the ceremony, and find a church organist to play the wedding march. Archie's father and a friend of Agatha acted as witnesses.

After a two-day honeymoon, Archie returned to duty and Agatha returned home to Ashfield. For another year, Agatha and Archie lived separate lives. Archie came home on leave only twice the whole year. Meanwhile, Agatha had been offered a job in the hospital dispensary—the department that prepared and dispensed medicine.

Working in the dispensary was often boring and tedious. But Agatha found that she had an interest in drugs— the plants they came from, their effects on the body, and their healing properties. Agatha decided to obtain her license as a chemist.

Agatha also thought for the first time about writing a mystery novel. With her innate curiosity about people and her love of puzzles and suspense, this seemed like a natural choice. She had grown up reading mysteries. One day she remembered a conversation she'd had with her sister Madge a few months earlier. After reading a classic mystery novel called *The Mystery of the Yellow Room,* Agatha commented to her sister Madge that she would like to try her hand at writing a detective novel. Madge responded by challenging Agatha to write one in which the reader couldn't guess the murderer.

Agatha thought about this. She knew that the most exciting story was one with a murderer whom the reader least suspects. "The whole point was that it must be somebody obvious but at the same time, for some reason, you would then find that it was not obvious, that he could not possibly have done it. But really of course he had," she wrote.

One day while riding the train home from work and mulling over ideas for her mystery novel, Agatha's curiosity was aroused by a husband and wife sitting across the train from her. She began to speculate on the life of this couple— their past, their occupations. What if the man were actually planning to murder his beloved wife? How could he do it so effectively as to "almost" get away with it? How could he pull off the "perfect crime?"

Agatha knew that no crime goes uninvestigated. Who would be the detective to solve this mystery? She was devoted to Sherlock Holmes—but her detective had to be different. Agatha decided her detective would be from another country. He would be clever and would love details. His investigative work would be so well crafted that it would be an art.

Thus Hercule Poirot was born. As Agatha described him, "He was hardly five feet, four inches, but carried himself with great dignity. His head was exactly the shape of an egg, and he always perched it a little on one side. His moustache was very stiff and military. The neatness of his attire was almost incredible. I believe a speck of dust would have caused him more pain than a bullet wound."

Poirot had a favorite saying: "The true work is done from within. The little gray cells—remember always the little gray cells!"

Agatha needed a location for her story. She created a place based on a village in northern England she had once passed through; a little town where everyone knew each other's business. Agatha named it Styles St. Mary in Essex. She called her new book *The Mysterious Affair at Styles.*

Once she had determined the plot, characters, location, detective, and title, Agatha began to write her story. Toward the middle of the book, Agatha felt blocked. She suddenly didn't like the plot and was unhappy with her characters. Clara saved the day, as she had before. She suggested that Agatha take a brief vacation so she could work on her book without interruption.

Agatha traveled by train to Dartmoor, a country village in the northern part of England. She stayed at the Moorland Hotel. It was a slightly gloomy place, but remote enough to give Agatha the solitude that she required.

> It was a large, dreary hotel with plenty of rooms. There were few people staying there. I don't think I spoke to any of them—it would have taken my mind away from what I was doing. I used to write laboriously all morning till my hand ached. Then I would have lunch, reading a book. Afterwards I would go out for a good walk on the moor, perhaps for a couple of hours. . . . As I walked, I muttered to myself, enacting the chapter that I was next going to write. . . . I would come home, have dinner, fall into bed and sleep for about twelve hours. Then I would get up and write passionately again all morning.

Peter Ustinov brought detective Hercule Poirot to life in several movies based on Agatha's books.

Agatha had completed the first draft of her novel by the time she returned home. She spent the next few weeks rewriting and editing her book until she felt that it was ready to send to a publisher.

Five publishers read and rejected Agatha's book, but Agatha wouldn't give up. She believed that her novel was good, and she knew that eventually someone would like it. She was right. Bodley Head, a London publisher, sent a letter asking Agatha to come and meet with the editors. Finally! Agatha was ecstatic.

In London, Bodley Head's publisher, John Lane, told Agatha that he wanted to publish her book. He pushed a contract in front of her and asked her to sign it. In her excitement, Agatha didn't take time to read what she was signing. Consequently she signed a contract that gave her publisher a financial advantage but left little for herself. Agatha earned only $100 from her first book. Luckily, she wasn't writing to become rich. She simply loved to write. Her head swam with plots and characters that just had to be put down on paper.

After being apart for two years, Archie sent Agatha some good news—he was being transferred to England! They could now make a real home for themselves. Agatha found a tiny one-bedroom apartment in London for them.

Although Agatha and Archie were finally living together, Agatha was often lonely. Archie had little time to spend with his wife. His work at the Air Ministry sometimes crept into the night, and Agatha spent a great deal of time by herself. Since she no longer lived near the hospital, Agatha had to give up her job at the dispensary. Believing that it would be easier to find a job as a secretary than as a chemist, she decided to go to secretarial school.

On November 11, 1918, Agatha walked out into the street during her lunch hour. She saw the street fill with people, all of them laughing, crying, and hugging each other. An armistice had just been declared with Germany. World War I was over.

Brothers, sons, and husbands would soon return from the battlefront. For Agatha, the end of the war meant that she and Archie could begin a normal married life together.

Agatha at age 32

❧ FOUR ❧

Life during Peacetime

1919–1926

In the early months of 1919, Agatha learned that she was pregnant. Their tiny apartment would be too small for three. Luckily, Agatha and Archie found a larger apartment in the same building. Archie had obtained a job in London. His salary was barely enough to live on. But Agatha also received a small amount of money from a trust fund left to her by her grandfather. The couple found that they could live comfortably combining these two incomes.

One day Agatha was busy decorating her new home when she received a call from John Lane at Bodley Head. It had been two years since she had signed her contract and *The Mysterious Affair at Styles* had not yet been published. Mr. Lane told Agatha that he wanted to change the ending of the book. He thought that it wasn't believable enough. Agatha agreed to rewrite the last chapter, changing it from a courtroom scene to a conversation in the library between Hercule Poirot and his colleague Hastings. Agatha had just sent the revision back to John Lane when she gave birth to a baby girl. It was August 5, 1919. She and Archie named their daughter Rosalind.

Ashfield was getting more expensive to maintain every year. Archie suggested that Clara sell the estate, but Agatha wouldn't hear of it. She had to find a way to earn some extra money and still be able to stay home with Rosalind. Agatha

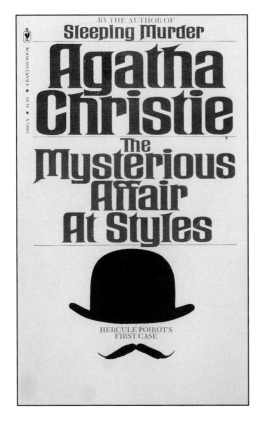

Agatha's first book, The Mysterious Affair at Styles, *introduced Hercule Poirot to the world.*

believed that if she wrote another book, she might be able to save Ashfield.

With encouragement from her husband, Agatha began to write her second book, *The Secret Adversary.* This book was published in 1922, one year after *The Mysterious Affair at Styles. The Secret Adversary* earned Agatha even less than her first work. She received another job, however, that made up for the loss. The editor of a magazine called *Sketch* offered Agatha a handsome sum of money to write a series of Hercule Poirot stories. Agatha spent much of the next year writing these stories, raising Rosalind, and working on a third novel, *Murder on the Links.*

One day Archie came home with a surprise. A man named Belcher, whom he had met some years before, had asked Archie to join him on a business trip to Australia, New Zealand, and South Africa. Belcher wanted to interest international businesspeople in a London trade show scheduled for 1924.

Archie had a big decision to make. If he accepted the offer, he would lose his job. Agatha saw the trip as a once-in-a-lifetime opportunity, however, and she encouraged him to accept. Belcher offered to pay for both Archie's and Agatha's expenses and to add a trip to Hawaii as a bonus.

Agatha was excited. She had always loved to travel, and this trip promised to be enjoyable. But what about Rosalind? She was too young to travel such a distance. So Agatha told Madge that she was going to leave Rosalind with a hired nurse. Madge, who was now a war widow with a young child of her own, offered to take the baby. Agatha felt relieved. She could travel without worrying about Rosalind's safety, because she knew that her daughter would be in capable hands.

Agatha and Archie loved the beaches of South Africa.

On January 20, 1922, Agatha and Archie set sail on the ship RMS *Kildonan Castle.* The first few days at sea were dreadful for Agatha. She had the worst case of seasickness she had ever experienced. Eventually, Agatha began to feel better and was able to enjoy the remainder of the trip.

The first stop was Cape Town, South Africa. The beautiful white beaches, the sunshine, and especially the intense heat delighted Agatha after the cold, dreary English weather. She also learned a new water sport, "bathing with planks," or surfing. She and Archie fled from the crowds whenever possible to go surfing in South Africa's warm waters. Agatha's most exciting time, however, was spent at the Cape Town Museum. She was fascinated by the displays of prehistoric fossils, rock carvings, and wall paintings.

In the beginning of April, Archie and Agatha left Cape Town, traveling north to Rhodesia (now Zimbabwe and Zambia). They had crossed about half the distance when they were delayed in Pretoria, South Africa. A workers' revolution was taking place, blocking all travel. The dispute involved the wages paid to gold mine workers. Many dissatisfied workers went on strike and the situation soon turned violent. The town swarmed with armored cars. Agatha and Archie could hear explosions from bombs in the distance.

It took almost a week for the army to put down the rebellion. During this time, Agatha and Archie prepared to continue on their travels through South Africa. Before setting out, however, they received a telegram from Major Belcher, who wanted them to return to Cape Town and join him aboard a ship bound for Australia.

When Agatha arrived in Cape Town, she found an envelope from Bodley Head waiting for her. The publisher had forwarded Agatha reviews of her second book, *The Secret Adversary*. Agatha nervously held her breath as she read them. They were all favorable! Relieved, Agatha wrote a hasty note to Bodley Head thanking them for sending her the good news. She also mailed a letter to Madge, asking her to write with news about Rosalind.

On April 9, Agatha and Archie sailed from Cape Town to Australia. When they arrived, Archie attended business meetings while Agatha spent hours at the local museum, examining skulls, skeletons, and ancient artifacts.

Agatha had brought along a small typewriter. Whenever she could snatch some time, she would spend it writing

Agatha and Rosalind

Hercule Poirot stories. These she sent off to the magazine *Sketch*. Agatha also mailed a collection of these stories to Bodley Head, hoping that they could be published as a book.

Agatha and Archie briefly parted ways after spending two weeks in Hawaii together. Archie went to Canada to finish some business while Agatha visited with her Aunt Cassie in New York City. When Archie joined her at the end of November, Agatha was anxious to return home. She sorely missed her mother, Madge, and three-year-old Rosalind.

After a six-day journey by ship from New York City to Southampton, England, Archie and Agatha took a train to Sussex. Both were glad to be home again.

Agatha was a caring mother, but she did not believe in giving up her career to raise a child. She wanted some time to write. While Archie went from one company to another looking for a job, Agatha spent her days finding blocks of time to write, as well as cook, clean, and care for Rosalind. Her next book was called *The Man in the Brown Suit.*

Agatha was rapidly gaining fame as a mystery novelist. One day she received a letter from *The Evening News,* a local publication. They wanted serial rights to *The Man in the Brown Suit.* A chapter of the book would appear in each issue of the magazine. Agatha received 500 pounds (about $400) for the chapters. She was thrilled. What should she do with this extra money? Buy a new wardrobe or some toys for Rosalind? Archie gave her a suggestion. Why not buy a car?

Agatha took Archie up on his suggestion and bought herself a gray Morris Cowley. Owning a car gave Agatha a

Her car gave Agatha a welcomed sense of independence.

kind of freedom that many women in 1923 could only dream about. It was unusual for a woman to drive a car, much less own one.

Archie supported Agatha's independence. If she had more freedom, then he could pursue his own interests. As the months went on, Agatha found herself more and more on her own. Archie spent most of his free time playing golf with friends. Agatha appreciated the extra time she had for her writing, but she was often lonely.

In 1925, at the age of thirty-five, Agatha wrote *The Murder of Roger Ackroyd,* a novel that marked a turning point in her career. Almost everyone began talking about the book. Agatha had fooled readers by adding an extremely surprising plot twist—the kind of possibility that hadn't occurred to even the most dedicated mystery lovers. Some critics said that Agatha had fooled readers deliberately, in order to point out their stupidity. Others applauded her technique as clever and brilliant. London's *Weekly Times* published a scathing review, calling the book "a tasteless and unfortunate let-down by a writer we had grown to admire." Agatha was undisturbed. A few reviewers' negative opinions were not important to her. She waited to see how many copies of her new book sold. *The Murder of Roger Ackroyd* became immensely popular from all the controversy.

In 1926 Agatha and Archie saw a house that they liked. Agatha fell in love with the gardens at first sight, although she was disappointed with the home's depressing interior. The previous owners had spent a lot of money on shiny bathroom fixtures but had paid little attention to the rest of the house.

The house was rumored to be unlucky. One couple who had lived there lost all their money. A few months after another couple moved into the house, the wife died. A third couple ended up getting a divorce. Agatha laughed at all this superstition, and she and Archie bought the house. They named it Styles, after Agatha's first book.

Maintaining the house soon became a financial burden, however. Agatha and Archie had a cook, a maid, and a butler. They also owned two cars. Worry about their dwindling bank account was soon diverted by something even more important. Clara Miller was seriously ill.

Agatha went to stay at Ashfield to be with Clara, who

Agatha and Archie named their house Styles after Agatha's first book.

was struggling with a severe case of bronchitis. Madge and Agatha took turns nursing their mother, but her health did not improve. In 1926, at the age of 72, Clara died.

Agatha grieved her mother's death for a long time. She and Clara had been very close and Agatha would sorely miss her. Agatha became depressed and distant. Archie had a difficult time handling the change that had come over his wife. He asked her to come to Spain with him on a business trip, but Agatha declined the offer. Instead, she returned to Ashfield and in a frenzy started to sort through her mother's belongings.

Tired and overworked, Agatha was on the verge of physical collapse. Archie refused to join her at Ashfield on the weekends. He did not want to miss his golf games. When Agatha saw Archie in August for their daughter's seventh birthday, he seemed like a stranger. In fact, Archie had some startling news. He had fallen in love with another woman and wanted a divorce.

The news was devastating for Agatha. First she had lost her mother, now her husband. She was unable to eat or sleep for days. She did nothing but cry. Her whole world seemed to have fallen apart.

In December 1926, Agatha told her secretary, Carlo, to take the day off. She encouraged Carlo to go out with friends and have a good time. Aware of Agatha's distress, Carlo at first refused—but Agatha insisted that she would be fine. In the evening, Carlo phoned Agatha to check on her. Agatha again told her not to worry. She would expect her on the last train.

When Carlo arrived home, however, the servants anxiously met her at the door. They told Carlo that Mrs. Christie had left the house at about eleven o'clock without telling anyone where she was going, and she hadn't yet returned. This behavior was so unlike Agatha that they were sure something was wrong. Agatha did not return to the house that night or the next morning. She had disappeared!

Police found Agatha's car abandoned after she was reported missing.

🎰 FIVE 🎰

A Mysterious Disappearance

1927–1929

Agatha's strange disappearance created real concern among her fans. England's beloved mystery writer had disappeared without a trace, and no one had a clue to her whereabouts. Was she a murder victim? Had she taken her own life? Had an overzealous fan kidnapped her?

The day after Agatha's disappearance, her car was found near a small lake called the Silent Pool a few miles from her house. Agatha's fur coat lay on the backseat along with a suitcase containing some of her clothes.

Scotland Yard, the largest police force in England, was not in the habit of getting involved in all crimes. Agatha was a very important person, however, and her disappearance was serious enough to warrant their efforts.

The detectives from Scotland Yard speculated that Agatha had been in a car accident and might have sustained head injuries. They thought that she could be wandering dazed and injured in the surrounding woods. The police organized search parties, asking for volunteers. Within two days, more than 15,000 citizens turned out to aid the search.

Small planes flew over the area in the hope of spotting Agatha's body. Packs of bloodhounds also helped in the search, sniffing out the woods within 100 miles of Agatha's house. The police used heavy machinery to dredge the Silent Pool.

The local newspaper published the latest photo of Agatha with this caption: *"The Daily News* offers £100 reward to the first person furnishing us with information leading to the discovery of the whereabouts, if alive, of Mrs. Christie."

The Silent Pool

Police used bloodhounds to search for the missing writer.

When the police questioned Agatha's servants, they learned of the Christies' troubled marriage. The police questioned Archie extensively. Although they sent him home, they monitored his phone calls and followed him to his office. Archie had become a suspect in Agatha's disappearance.

Hundreds of calls flooded the local police station and Scotland Yard. Callers claimed to have seen a woman fitting Agatha's description in locations that were miles apart. Then, on December 14, 1926, ten days after Agatha disappeared, the police received yet another call. This call was different from the others. Someone had recognized Agatha from the newspaper photo. The caller had seen her in the dining room of the Hydropathic Hotel, a health spa in Yorkshire. Apparently, Agatha had registered at the hotel under

Agatha was finally found at a spa called the Hydropathic Hotel.

the name of Teresa Neele and had been there for ten days. Archie arrived at the hotel to find Agatha in a strange state. She hardly recognized him.

Many stories circulated to explain Agatha's odd behavior. Archie told the newspapers that his wife had had an accident and that she was suffering from amnesia. Agatha's fans were skeptical. The fact that Agatha had a packed suitcase in her car seemed to indicate that she had left deliberately. But why hadn't she told anybody? She was not the kind of person who would purposely cause her friends and family to worry. Did Agatha have a mental breakdown due to stress? In her confused state did she think that she had planned the trip to Yorkshire?

Some people thought that Agatha had deliberately staged her disappearance to draw attention to herself. But those who knew Agatha knew that nothing could be further from the truth. She had always been very shy. She had difficulty with her growing fame and usually refused interviews to reporters and writers.

Agatha remained silent on the subject of her disappearance. This caused even greater speculation. The fact that she refused even to comment on the subject made people feel that there could be a deeper mystery. But Agatha never told anyone the real story behind her strange vanishing.

Agatha remained in seclusion for several weeks after she returned to Styles. As the new year began, Agatha knew she couldn't avoid certain problems in her life any longer. She accepted the fact that her marriage was over. Agatha hoped that this acceptance might help to heal her broken heart. Agatha also needed to face her financial problems. Money continued to run low, and Agatha had to support both herself and Rosalind. Agatha knew that writing again would help her, but she couldn't concentrate. She was terribly distracted by her emotional and financial burdens.

Agatha decided to take several Hercule Poirot stories and put them into one book. She titled this collection *The Big Four.* Agatha followed this with *The Mystery of the Blue Train.* Desperate for money, she forced herself to write the novel. "I have always hated *The Mystery of the Blue Train,* but I got it written, and sent off to the publishers. It sold just as well as my last book had done. So I had to content myself with that—though I cannot say I have ever been proud of it."

Agatha's secretary, Carlo, with Rosalind

The year 1927 was a time of healing for Agatha. With eight-year-old Rosalind in boarding school, Agatha had a lot of time on her hands. At first she was overwhelmed by being a single woman again. As the year came to an end, however, she felt the desire to write returning to her. Doing something creative helped her to feel better about herself. By early 1928, Agatha was busy writing short stories for magazines. Encouraged by her renewed ability to write, she began a new novel, *The Seven Dials Mystery.*

Every writer has a unique way of beginning a book. Agatha began hers by jotting down notes in anything available—old diaries, notepads, or composition books. "Plots come to me at such odd moments; when I am walking along a street, or examining a hat shop with particular interest, suddenly a splendid idea comes into my head, and I think, 'Now that would be a neat way of covering up the crime so that nobody would see the point.' Of course, all the practical details are still to be worked out, and the people have to creep slowly into my consciousness."

Agatha began by titling a fresh page, "New Book." Then she wrote down six important questions: *Who* committed the murder? *What* was the motive? *When* and *where* did the murder take place? *Why* was the person murdered? And finally, *how* was the person murdered?

By the end of 1928, Agatha was working on several writing projects at once. Her books continued to sell well. With

After a traumatic year adjusting to her new life as a single woman, Agatha began writing novels again, starting with The Seven Dials Mystery.

the money she earned from the sale of her books and stories, along with a stipend that Archie sent her every month, Agatha could meet her living expenses.

In one of Agatha's new projects, *The Murder at the Vicarage,* she introduced a new fictional detective—Miss Jane Marple. Miss Marple was different from Hercule Poirot. She was a demure, elderly lady who lived in the fictitious village of St. Mary Mead.

Agatha's memories of the elderly women who had gossiped with her grandmother at Ealing were surely the basis for Miss Marple. Jane Marple was exceedingly proper. She had an uncanny knack for knowing things about people upon first meeting them. Miss Marple believed that almost everyone—herself excepted—had a dark side. Agatha wrote: "There was no unkindness in Miss Marple, she just did not trust people. Though she expected the worst, she often accepted people kindly in spite of what they were."

In *The Murder at the Vicarage,* Miss Marple demonstrates her astute powers of observation, her knack for detecting dishonesty, and her remarkable ability to solve a crime. Her quiet, unassuming air fools people into believing that she is merely a doddering old woman.

At thirty-eight, Agatha began to realize that she could function very well without a husband. She felt strong and completely able to take care of herself. Agatha wanted to test these new feelings. She decided to take a trip to the West Indies with her secretary, Carlo. Agatha wanted to see how comfortable she would be traveling on her own with another woman for companionship.

While vacationing, Agatha became friendly with a couple

In The Murder at the Vicarage, *Agatha introduced Jane Marple, a clever elderly woman. Miss Marple is played here by Joan Hickson in a television version of the book.*

who had traveled extensively. They told Agatha and Carlo stories of the Middle East—Baghdad, Istanbul, and Cairo. They also told her about a unique mode of travel—a train that traveled the whole expanse of Europe and the Middle East. The train—called the Orient Express—was like a hotel on wheels.

To Agatha this sounded like a marvelous way to see the world. She hadn't a moment to lose. Anxious to experience

The Orient Express became Agatha's favorite mode of travel.

the thrill of riding on the Orient Express, Agatha rushed to a travel agent the next morning to buy a ticket. She would travel to Turkey, Syria, and Iraq. She was wildly excited.

This time Agatha wanted to travel alone. She was nervous, but she knew that if she gave in to her fears, she might never have the courage to do anything like this again. Five days after arriving home from the West Indies, Agatha boarded the Orient Express.

Belgian businessman Georges Nagelmackers had created the Orient Express in 1893. He wanted to design a train so luxurious that it would be compared to the finest hotels in Europe. The train had crystal chandeliers, marble bath fixtures, velvet upholstery, and the finest bed linens that money could buy.

Four train systems ran in the Orient Express line. All of them began in Paris, but they each traveled a different route across Europe. The train that Agatha took was called the Simplon-Orient Express. From Paris, this train traveled through Switzerland, Italy, Austria, Yugoslavia, Bulgaria, and Turkey.

Agatha loved the train's luxurious decor, and she met many fascinating people on the trip. Like her fellow passengers, Agatha had a private car for sleeping. She ate her meals with the rest of the guests in a formal dining car. Here, waiters dressed in starched white shirts and black suits attended to each passenger. Agatha spent her days reading, chatting, or playing cards and checkers with the other passengers. Sometimes she simply sat and watched the countryside pass by.

Agatha wrote about some of the scenery she viewed from the train. "Here was the fascination of looking out at an entirely different world: going through the mountain gorges,

Agatha was fascinated by the sights of Baghdad.

watching ox-carts and picturesque wagons, studying groups of people on station platforms, getting out occasionally at places like Nish and Belgrade and seeing the large engines changed and new monsters coming on."

When Agatha finally arrived in Istanbul, she was introduced to a group of English families that were staying in the same hotel. This did not please her, however. She had left England for the new and exotic. She had no wish to be with other English people. Agatha decided to travel on to Baghdad, the capital of Iraq.

She began her journey to Baghdad by first crossing the Bosporus Sea by ferry and then continuing by train to Damascus, Syria. She stayed in Damascus for three days and then boarded a bus for the trek into the desert. After a two-day journey on a hot and smelly bus, she finally arrived in Baghdad.

After settling into her hotel, Agatha arranged for a visit to the excavations at Ur. Ur had once been the center of the ancient Sumerian civilization, dating back to the fourth century B.C. The Sumerians were known for the canals they had constructed to connect their cities. Agatha was fascinated by their ancient history. She had read of the exploits of a famous archaeologist, Leonard Woolley, and she hoped that he would allow her to explore some of his excavations.

Fortunately, Katharine Woolley, who had accompanied her husband to Ur, was a great fan of Agatha Christie. Agatha was treated as an honored guest at the archaeological dig. She gained admittance to parts of the excavation normally off-limits to tourists.

Archaeologist Leonard Woolley

*The Woolley's excavation at Ur. Katharine Woolley is pictured in
the lower left center.*

Agatha remained with the Woolleys for several weeks
before returning to Baghdad. In November 1929, Agatha decided to return home for Christmas. Katharine Woolley
wouldn't let her leave, however, without extracting a promise
that Agatha would return in the spring.

When Agatha returned to England, she quickly resumed her normal writing schedule. Her first task was to
finish *Black Coffee,* a play she had started before her trip. A

classic spy thriller featuring Hercule Poirot, *Black Coffee* concerned a scientist who discovered the formula for a deadly explosive but was killed and robbed of it. The three-act play went over quite well in local theaters.

In addition to writing a play, Agatha made another departure from mystery writing. She decided to write a non-mystery novel and publish it under a pseudonym. She called her novel *Giant's Bread* and published it under the name Mary Westmacott. "It had been exciting to begin with, to be writing books.... What I wanted to do now was to write something other than a detective story. So, with a rather guilty feeling, I enjoyed myself writing a straight novel called *Giant's Bread....* I used the name of Mary Westmacott, and nobody knew that it was written by me," she wrote.

Agatha found valuable time to write while on an expedition at Ninevah (above) with Max.

❧ SIX ❧

A World Traveler

1930–1933

In the spring of 1930, at the age of forty, Agatha made good on her promise to Katharine Woolley. Once again Agatha boarded the Orient Express bound for Turkey. Her destination, of course, was the Woolley's excavation at Ur.

When she arrived at the dig, Agatha met another member of the team, twenty-five-year-old Max Mallowan. Max and Agatha immediately struck up a friendship. Although there was a fifteen-year difference in their ages, Max found Agatha to be an intelligent conversationalist and a pleasant companion. Agatha was impressed by Max's knowledge of a wide variety of topics.

After staying with the Woolleys for a few weeks, Agatha wanted to travel back to Baghdad and then on to Greece. Max decided to accompany Agatha since he was also on his way to Greece. With Max as a guide, Agatha learned much about the ancient ruins and their history. She and Max also learned a lot about each other. Agatha marveled that Max was so easy to talk to. She had never met anyone quite like him.

Archaeologist Max Mallowan and Agatha

Max and Agatha had agreed to spend a few days in Baghdad before traveling to Greece. But Agatha received a telegram as soon as she arrived at her hotel. Twelve-year-old Rosalind was very sick with pneumonia.

Agatha was frantic, especially when she found out that it would take at least four days to return to London by train. To make matters worse, she fell and sprained her ankle. Max came to the rescue. He volunteered to travel back to London with Agatha. When she protested, Max pointed out that with her sprained ankle, she would need someone to carry her luggage. Besides, he continued, a traveling companion might help keep Agatha's mind off her worries.

Four days later Agatha arrived in England, relieved to find that Rosalind was greatly improved. She immediately took Rosalind to Ashfield to recuperate. Max went to

London on business. A few weeks later, Agatha invited Max to spend the weekend at Ashfield. Before he left on Sunday afternoon, Max asked Agatha to marry him.

Agatha was surprised and delighted, yet hesitant. Even though he was more mature and serious than most men his age, Max was so much younger than she. Agatha was afraid of being hurt a second time. She wanted to be sure about this before saying yes. Agatha decided to go on a short trip to think things over. She took Rosalind and Carlo to the Isle of Skye, off the coast of southern England.

Agatha felt that she had been neglecting her daughter, and the week gave them time to renew their relationship.

The Isle of Skye. Agatha traveled here to think about marrying Max.

Agatha also came to an important decision on this trip. She would marry Max.

Max and Agatha were married on September 11, 1930. Their honeymoon took them to Italy and Greece. Six weeks later, pleasantly weary of traveling and sightseeing, Agatha and Max realized that they had to get back to work. Max had promised Leonard Woolley that he would spend another five months working on the excavation at Ur. While Agatha prepared to return to England, Max journeyed to Turkey. They would be separated for five months, but Agatha knew that she would have enough to do to fill the time until they were together again.

Agatha had trouble finding time to write again after all that had happened. She and Max had purchased a new house. She had decorating and shopping to do, and daily letters to write to Max. Agatha also decided to take lessons in drawing and clay sculpture. But in early December, Agatha attended a meeting of the Detection Club and was thrust back into her work.

Members of the Detection Club dedicated themselves to upholding the highest standards of mystery writing. Membership was by invitation only. The members of the club included well-known British mystery writers such as Dorothy Sayers and Anthony Berkeley. The members met regularly over dinner at a posh London restaurant. At one particular dinner, Dorothy Sayers proposed that the members write a radio series for the British Broadcasting Corporation (BBC).

Sayers told Detection Club members that there would be twelve broadcasts in the production. Each member would

DOROTHY L. SAYERS

British mystery writer Dorothy Sayers was well known for her fictional sleuth Lord Peter Wimsey. Sayers and Agatha both belonged to the Detection Club.

write two. Agatha was given the task of writing the second and fourth episodes of the mystery series, called *The Scoop*. The story concerned a newspaper reporter who discovers important information and is murdered because of the discovery.

A mystery novel is challenge enough for an author working alone, but with six authors, each with a different style and different ideas, the difficulty is even greater. Dorothy Sayers had the thankless task of coordinating the writers. She tried to smooth out differences in the authors' personalities and keep everyone on schedule.

Despite the complications, *The Scoop* was a broadcasting success. Working on the series also reminded Agatha that she was a writer first and a homemaker second. She had missed writing on a regular basis. Agatha promised herself that she would start to write again and would never stop.

Her next novel was a Hercule Poirot mystery called *Peril at End House*. Poirot helps a young woman uncover the secrets of a sinister mansion, End House, which she has inherited from her uncle. Agatha also wrote a collection of short stories featuring Miss Marple.

In March 1931, Agatha joined Max at Ur. They would travel home together when he finished the excavation. Max had told Leonard Woolley that he would no longer be working with him. Max wanted Agatha to be with him on all future digs, and he worried that Katharine Woolley would make Agatha's life miserable.

Almost as soon as Max and Agatha returned to England, Max had to leave for another dig. This time he was excavating at Nineveh in Iraq. Agatha promised to join him as soon as she could find someone to rent their house.

In October Agatha packed up her typewriter and joined Max at Nineveh. She couldn't stay long. She wanted to return home for Christmas because Rosalind would be home from school. Agatha decided to return home via her favorite mode of transportation, the Orient Express.

Agatha's journey home was not as pleasant as her previous experiences on the famous train. Soon after the Orient Express left the station, a violent storm broke out. The train came to a halt. Agatha and the other passengers learned that one of the train crossings was flooded. Fuel was low and the train grew chilly. Passengers received blankets and hot tea to make them more comfortable.

Agatha and the other passengers eventually transferred to a new train, but they had no food or water. All the baggage got terribly mixed up, and Agatha couldn't find her luggage. And the adventure wasn't over.

Snow fell during the night, just as the train reached Sofia, Bulgaria. The train became marooned in the deep drifts. Agatha and her fellow passengers grew hungrier and colder, and their spirits sagged. After seven hours, they were finally rescued by another train, and the trip resumed without incident.

Agatha had developed a talent for turning a negative experience into something positive. Her difficult trip home was no exception. She took elements of her adventures and used them for a new mystery novel. *Murder on the Orient Express,* another book featuring Hercule Poirot, became one of the most famous mystery novels of the century. The passengers are colorful and eccentric and not always who they seem to be.

In 1932 Agatha wrote three new novels and worked with members of the Detection Club on another book. In April 1933, Max received a commission to lead an archaeological expedition in Iraq, and he asked Agatha to join him. Once again, Agatha packed her typewriter and lots of pencils and paper along with her clothing. She didn't want to waste a minute.

Max found Agatha to be an indispensable member of his team. In addition to cleaning and assembling broken pieces of pottery that members of the expedition dug up, Agatha also recorded important finds by sketching them into Max's notes.

Although Agatha helped her husband on the expedition, she was still able to write. She completed two mystery novels, a collection of short stories, and another Mary Westmacott novel before she and Max left Nineveh ten months later.

Agatha set her novel Appointment with Death *in the Middle Eastern city of Petra (above).*

❧ SEVEN ❧

An Amateur Archaeologist
1934–1938

By 1934 Agatha owned two houses in addition to Ashfield. She had always loved houses, and owning and decorating a new house was her favorite pastime. "What I liked playing with as a child, I like playing with as an adult. I have liked playing Houses, for instance. I can see plainly now that I have continued to play houses ever since. I have gone over innumerable houses, bought houses, exchanged them for other houses, furnished houses, decorated houses, made structural alterations to houses."

In December of 1934, Agatha and Max purchased Winterbrook, a splendid house in Wallingford in the Thames Valley. Agatha loved its large rooms and spacious garden. Agatha spent the next few months decorating Winterbrook and typing up her next three novels: *Death in the Clouds,* her first mystery novel to take place on an airplane; *The ABC Murders,* featuring Hercule Poirot; and *Three Act Tragedy.*

In February 1935, Agatha and Max left cold, damp Wallingford for Chagar Bazar, a new dig site outside

Beirut, Lebanon. Housing on an expedition often consisted of several tents pitched in the desert, but this time Max wanted to have a house built. They would be working at this dig site for a long time, and he and Agatha wanted to be comfortable.

Finding builders was easy. Almost all the men from nearby villages were out of work. Some of the crew worked on the actual construction of the house while others built furnishings, such as tables, desks, chairs, shelves, beds, dressers, and even toilet seats.

During the construction, Max and Agatha had arranged to rent a house owned by a wealthy Iraqi man. He had agreed to have the house cleaned and painted for Max and Agatha.

When they arrived at the rental house, however, they found it filled with seven families and all of their animals. Max tried to explain to the people that he and Agatha had paid to rent the house. After a great deal of fighting and screaming, Max appealed to his assistant, Hamoudi, to deal with the situation. Hamoudi went directly to the village priest and asked for his help. A couple hours later, Agatha and Max watched as angry men and weeping women and children streamed into the courtyard, followed by hens, goats, cats, and dogs.

When Max and Agatha finally entered the house, it was filthy. Hamoudi cleared and partially cleaned one room so that they could all get some sleep. Agatha and Max settled gratefully into their cots. But after a short time, Agatha awoke with the feeling that something was running back and forth across her bed. At first, she ignored it—but then she felt something run across her face. She turned on the kerosene lamp next to her cot and realized with horror that the room was filled with mice. "They run gaily over our beds, squeaking as they run. Mice across one's face, mice tweaking your hair—mice! Mice! MICE! . . . Horrible! The walls are covered with strange, pale, crawling cockroach-like creatures! A mouse is sitting on the foot of my bed attending to his whiskers! Horrible things are crawling everywhere!"

Max woke up long enough to try to calm Agatha. He told her that if she went back to sleep, nothing would bother her. He demonstrated this by rolling over and falling back to sleep, as mice and roaches crawled all over his cot. Agatha tried to follow his advice and did fall asleep briefly, ". . . but little feet running across my face wake me up. I flash on the light. The cockroaches have increased, and a large black spider is descending upon me from the ceiling!"

Nearly hysterical, Agatha took her cot into the courtyard, where she fell asleep almost immediately.

The next morning Hamoudi told Max and Agatha that he could solve the problem. He brought a cat from one of the nearby villages. This was no ordinary cat. He was a professional. "Whilst we dine, it crouches in ambush behind a packing crate. Five times during the meal a mouse emerges and runs across the floor, and five times our cat springs. The cat stays with us five days. After those five days no mice appear. The cat then leaves us, and the mice never come back," Agatha wrote.

News of work traveled quickly throughout the nearby villages. As soon as Max and Agatha arrived at the dig site in Chagar Bazar, they faced dozens of men seeking employment. Max tried to find out which men were qualified in carpentry. Those who had building experience he assigned to

Hamoudi, who supervised construction. Max directed the remaining men to begin digging for artifacts at the site.

At the end of each day, workers approached Max with their finds. He discarded pieces that he didn't consider valuable, while he gently placed those of value in a box. Agatha recorded each worker's name in a journal, along with the amount he should be paid.

Every day Agatha carefully cleaned all the artifacts that Max had received the day before. She gently brushed off each piece, removing any sand or debris. She "catalogued" the pieces—entering a description of each artifact in a journal and assigning it a number. Then the pieces were packed carefully in a special case.

Max and Agatha only stayed in Chagar Bazar for a couple months. They would return again in the fall when the new house was complete. Agatha was anxious to go back to England in time for spring. Her gardens would be blooming, and she had pruning and planting to do. She also had a couple of new novels stirring inside her.

Her next book, *Murder in Mesopotamia,* had a setting similar to Ur—where Agatha had stayed with the Woolleys in 1930. Mesopotamia lies between the Tigris and Euphrates Rivers in Iraq. The novel features Hercule Poirot, who is asked to solve the murder of an archaeologist's wife.

In Agatha's next book, *Cards on the Table,* she gave readers a hint. The book's introduction stated that only four suspects could have committed the crime, and that the solution to this crime could be deduced by a reader familiar with the game of bridge.

In the fall of 1935, Agatha and Max returned to Chagar Bazar. They settled comfortably into their new home and went to work. Max discovered that he had chosen a perfect site for digging. One afternoon, as Max reviewed the artifacts that had been uncovered during the course of the day, a worker approached with a stone slab in his hand. Max couldn't believe his eyes. He quickly asked the worker where he had been digging. Max directed all the workers to begin digging there immediately. Although the sun had grown hot and it was time to rest, Max had to see if there were other pieces of stone like this one. This was no ordinary slab of stone. It was part of a tablet that the ancient Assyrians had used to write on.

By the time the digging season was over, Max and his workers had uncovered seventy similar stone tablets. The tablets had to be put together like a jigsaw puzzle. After he sent them to a museum in Cairo for inspection, Max learned that the tablets dated to the year 1800 B.C. They were nearly 4,000 years old.

These cylindrical seals (right) were rolled to form impressions (left). The bottom seal was found at Chagar Bazar and is almost 4,000 years old.

Agatha learned a great deal about archaeology while working at Chagar Bazar. She got up early each morning and prepared tea and breakfast. She then worked alongside Max in the morning sun, helping him direct the workers, and collecting, cleaning, and cataloguing artifacts. Each afternoon, when the sun grew unbearably hot, Agatha would spend time helping Max piece together the stone tablets. Then she would sit down at her writing table and work on her next novel. During this busy time, she wrote one of her most famous mysteries, *Death on the Nile.*

In writing *Death on the Nile,* Agatha drew upon her love for Egypt, which had begun years earlier when she and her mother spent time in Cairo. Agatha had always been fascinated with the steamers that traveled up and down the Nile River. These long, flat-bottomed boats had two or three decks and were mostly used by tourists. Agatha set *Death on the Nile* on one of these steamers. Each of its eccentric passengers holds a grudge against the murder victim. Of course, Hercule Poirot happens to be vacationing with the other passengers and is asked to solve the crime.

In the spring of 1937, nineteen-year-old Rosalind went on her first expedition. Max was digging at a new location, Tell Brak in Syria, as well as at Chagar Bazar. Rosalind quickly learned how to assist on a dig. Her sketches proved to be especially helpful. Now Agatha had more time for her writing. She was anxious to begin a new novel. She had been jotting down notes for a couple months. It was time to start writing *Appointment with Death.*

Agatha set this novel in Petra, a city near Jordan in the Middle East. Although Petra has a unique landscape, Agatha spent little time describing it in her novel. Agatha rarely spent much time on descriptions, except those necessary to the plot. Many readers who disliked lengthy descriptions enjoyed this feature of Agatha's novels. Others criticized Agatha for not spending more time depicting her settings.

By the end of 1938, Agatha had completed another novel, *A Holiday for Murder.* She wrote this book in response to a remark from her brother-in-law, James, who told Agatha that her novels should have more blood in them. Agatha tried to get more "bloody" in this novel, but she found it difficult. Agatha had always been gentle in her handling of murder. She avoided graphic descriptions, leaving it up to the reader to envision the scene. Her violent murders were usually depicted by broken vases, overturned furniture, or smashed teacups.

Agatha also wrote a play during this time. *Akhnaton,* set in Egypt, is about the life of King Amenhotep III.

When Max and Agatha left Syria at the end of 1938, they both had a feeling that they might not return for a long time. Europe was in turmoil and people feared that another war would break out soon. Agatha was anxious to return to her home in England—a place she believed to be safe.

A publicity photo of Agatha, 1940

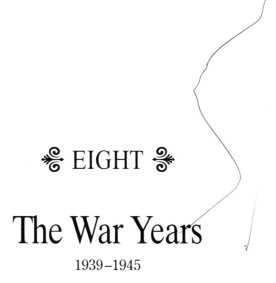

✖ EIGHT ✖

The War Years

1939–1945

When Agatha returned to England in 1939, she bought another new house—this time in Devon, near Torquay. Greenway House sat by itself on a hill surrounded by several acres of land. Max and Agatha settled in, and Agatha started to think of the books she wanted to write during the next year.

Meanwhile, talk of a major war filled the air. Germany, under the rule of Adolf Hitler, had begun a ruthless campaign to invade its European neighbors. On September 3, 1939, Agatha listened to the radio while she was preparing dinner. Suddenly the voice of Neville Chamberlain, the prime minister of England, interrupted the radio program. Chamberlain told listeners that Germany had invaded Poland two days before. France and Great Britain had promised to protect Poland. England had declared war on Germany.

Agatha remained relatively calm about the events. She had lived through one war; she believed she could live through another. Agatha thought the best way to deal with the situation was to continue living as normally as possible. So she kept writing—beginning with a new collection of short stories. *The Regatta Mystery* included stories featuring both Hercule Poirot and Miss Marple.

Agatha based her next mystery, *And Then There Were None,* on an English nursery rhyme:

> Ten little Indian boys went out to dine;
> One choked his little self and then there were Nine.
> Nine little Indian boys sat up very late;
> One overslept himself and then there were Eight....

The rhyme proceeds in this manner until the last stanza:

> One little Indian boy left all alone;
> He went and hanged himself and then there were None.

In this mystery, ten people are invited to a deserted island by a mysterious host. During their stay, each guest disappears and is found murdered. When the tenth is murdered, readers are left baffled, since the island is supposedly deserted. One review called this "one of the most ingenious thrillers in many a day."

All of England felt the effects of the war. People stood in line for hours, waiting for their share of rationed milk and bread. Air raids were common: sirens sounded when an enemy plane approached London. Everyone on the street ran to an underground shelter, remaining until the "all-clear" siren wailed. "Blackouts" helped protect the country from nighttime attacks. At dusk all streetlights, automobile lights, and outdoor house lights had to be extinguished. Blackouts made it difficult for the enemy planes to find their targets.

Most people stayed home at night. Agatha and Max spent their evenings reading by the light of a small lamp with all the shades pulled down. Agatha wrote during the day.

Her next novel, *One, Two, Buckle My Shoe,* was again based on a nursery rhyme. Each of the book's ten chapters corresponded to a line of the well-known verse:

> One, two, buckle my shoe,
> Three, four, shut the door,
> Five, six, pick up sticks,
> Seven, eight, lay them straight,
> Nine, ten, a good fat hen...

While Agatha wrote in Devon, the Germans bombed London regularly. Agatha learned of a campaign to evacuate London children to the countryside. She quickly got in touch with the War Department and offered her home as a shelter for the children.

She and Max continued to live at Greenway House for several months after the children arrived. Then Max went to

Children being evacuated from London to the British countryside during World War II.

London and volunteered to help with the war effort. Agatha applied for a job at the Devon hospital where she had worked during World War I. She told them about her experience in the dispensary years before and was hired immediately.

In the spring of 1940, Agatha and Rosalind moved to London to be with Max, who had accepted a job with the Air Force. Agatha and Max moved into Agatha's London house. One day when they were both away, the house was bombed. Agatha was upset by the loss, but she was grateful that she and Max hadn't been home. They moved to another part of London. Agatha found volunteer work in another hospital while Max prepared to go to the Middle East. This time, however, he wasn't going as an archaeologist but as an adviser on Arabian affairs. His knowledge of Arabic made him a valuable addition to the War Department.

Agatha missed Max terribly. She wrote to him every day and prayed for his safe return. She knew that she must keep busy until the war was over and Max was back home again. She threw herself into her writing. "I never found any difficulty in writing during the war, as some people did; I suppose because I cut myself off into a different compartment of my mind. I could live in the book among the people I was writing about, and mutter their conversations and see them striding about the room I had invented for them."

Despite bombs dropping around her and windows shattering from explosions, Agatha completed two novels in 1940: *Evil under the Sun* and *N or M?* When she had finished these books, Agatha decided to do something unusual. She wanted to write two books and dedicate them to the two most important people in her life, Rosalind and Max. *Sleeping Murder* would be Miss Marple's last case, and

Curtain would be Hercule Poirot's final case. Agatha did not want these books to be published until after her death. She locked the manuscripts in a vault. Only Max could have access to them.

Agatha continued to write during the next three years. She completed six more mystery novels and two plays. She also wrote another Mary Westmacott novel, *The Silent Spring,* about a woman who is stranded at a lonely hotel and forced to review her life. The woman realizes that she has not been the wonderful wife and mother that she thought she was. Agatha wrote *The Silent Spring* in three days. "I wrote the one book that has satisfied me completely....the book that I had always wanted to write, that had been clear in my mind....It is an odd feeling to have a book growing inside you, for perhaps six or seven years, knowing that one day you will write it, knowing that it is building up, all the time, to what it already is."

Agatha also finished her first nonfiction book. *Come, Tell Me How You Live* recounted her expeditions with Max in Syria and Turkey. In the book's foreword, Agatha explained the source of the book's title. "Tell me how you live" is the question that archaeologists ask of past civilizations. With picks and spades, Agatha explained, they find the answers: "These were our cooking pots. In this big silo we kept our grain. With these bone needles we sewed our clothes. These were our houses, this our bathroom, here our system of sanitation! Here, in this pot, are the gold earrings of my daughter's dowry."

World War II officially ended with Japan's surrender in September 1945. All of England rejoiced. Agatha and Max returned to Greenway House in Devon to rebuild their lives.

Agatha at home, 1946

✵ NINE ✵

After the War

1946–1949

In the days following the war's end, elation soon turned to exhaustion and depression for the British people. Hospitals, office buildings, stores, and houses had all been bombed. Food, fuel, and clean water had to be rationed. Every family received one loaf of bread and a bottle of milk to last for three days. Most people used bicycles and left their cars at home.

After Agatha and Max moved back to Greenway House, they, too, felt a need to recover from the difficulties of war. Since Agatha's books were selling well, she decided to spend a year just relaxing and fixing up her house. She and Max spent many quiet days together. Max worked on compiling his notes from various digs. Agatha worked in her garden, cooked for relatives and friends who came to visit, and caught up on her reading.

In 1947 Agatha received a call from the British Broadcasting Corporation. Queen Mary of England was preparing to celebrate her eightieth birthday. A great fan of Agatha's, the queen had read every book written by the novelist.

Queen Mary had a special request. She wanted Agatha to write a radio play in honor of her birthday. Although Agatha had said many years before that she would never again write anything for the BBC, she could not refuse the queen's request.

Agatha had recently heard a story about a young orphan who had been mistreated by the people he lived with. She based her radio play on this story, calling it *Three Blind Mice*. Agatha had fun naming her stories and plays after English nursery rhymes.

After the play's radio debut, many listeners wrote to the BBC to say how much they had enjoyed it. Queen Mary sent Agatha a thank-you note to show her appreciation for this special gift.

Agatha enjoyed writing plays as much as she enjoyed seeing them performed. "I find that writing plays is much more fun than writing books. For one thing, you need not worry about those long descriptions of places and people. And you must write quickly if only to keep the mood while it lasts and to keep the dialogue flowing naturally."

In 1947 Agatha wrote another mystery play, *The Hollow.* She took the title from a line in "Maud," a poem by Alfred Lord Tennyson: "I hate the dreadful hollow behind the little wood."

In the autumn of 1947, when Agatha was 57 years old, she and Max returned to the Middle East. Max had been

England's Queen Mary (above) loved Agatha's novels. Agatha wrote a special radio play in honor of the queen's eightieth birthday.

working as head of the archaeology department at the University of London. This position gave him time and money to teach, lecture, and conduct his research. He decided to travel to Baghdad to obtain permission to begin another dig.

Travel in the Middle East had become expensive since the war. Agatha's editor told her that he would advance her some money for the trip if she promised him another book—set in Baghdad. Agatha agreed to his proposal and immediately began work on *The House in Baghdad.*

Overall, traveling to the Middle East wasn't as much fun for Agatha as it had been before the war. The Orient Express had become too costly. She also missed the bus ride across the desert to Baghdad, for she and Max flew directly from London to Baghdad. Agatha wrote:

> I think nothing has disappointed me more in my life
> than the establishment of the aeroplane as a regular
> method of travel. Ships can still be romantic. As for
> trains—what can beat a train? Especially before the
> diesels and their smell arrived. A great puffing mon-
> ster carrying you through gorges and valleys, by
> waterfalls, past snow mountains, alongside country
> roads with strange peasants in carts...To travel by
> train is to see nature and human beings, towns and
> churches and rivers, in fact, to see life.

Before he could begin digging at Nimrud, the new site, Max had to negotiate with Iraqi authorities. After six months of negotiations in Baghdad, Max was finally given permission to dig.

In January 1949, Agatha joined Max at Nimrud. The couple occupied a wing of a house that belonged to a wealthy sheik. The mud-brick house had several rooms, but no bedroom. Agatha, Max, and two assistants all slept in tents. There wasn't much privacy, but they were happy.

Once Agatha had settled in, she began to work on a new book. She knew that when the dig began she would have little time for writing. She would be needed to clean, repair, photograph, label, and catalogue the artifacts.

During 1949, Agatha was frustrated because of some confusion over her tax status in the United States. As a British citizen, she believed that she was exempt from U.S. income tax. The United States government thought otherwise, however. Most of the money from the sale of her books in the United States was being held until the tax situation was resolved.

Agatha was also becoming increasingly unhappy about the covers and jackets of some of her books. She told her publisher that she didn't want the covers to reveal the plot or the solution to the mystery. Nor did she want any of her characters portrayed on the cover. After receiving several strongly worded letters to this effect, the publisher finally conceded to Agatha's wishes.

The final frustration came, however, when a reporter for the *Sunday Times* of London revealed Agatha's identity as Mary Westmacott. Agatha was furious, but there was little she could do. Her secret was out.

Agatha and Max on their way to Nimrud, 1950

❧ TEN ❧

Gifts to the World

1950–1976

In 1950, when Agatha and Max returned to Nimrud
following a stay in England, Agatha had a wonderful surprise
waiting for her.

> This year one more room has been added to the
> Expedition House, a room that measures about nine
> feet square. It has a plastered floor with rush mats
> and couple of gay coarse rugs. There is a picture on
> the wall by a young Iraqi artist.... There is a window
> looking out east towards the snow-topped mountains
> of Kurdistan. On the outside of the door is affixed a
> square card on which is printed in cuneiform BEIT
> AGATHA (Agatha's House).... So this is my "house"
> and the idea is that in it I have complete privacy and
> can apply myself seriously to the business of writ-
> ing.... I sit at a fairly firm wooden table, and beside
> me is a gaily painted tin box with which Arabs travel.
> In it I propose to keep my typescript as it progresses.

At the age of 60, Agatha wanted to try writing something different: her autobiography. "The urge to write one's autobiography, so I have been told, overtakes everyone sooner or later. It has suddenly overtaken me!"

This was also the year the BBC produced its first Agatha Christie television movie. Although television had been invented almost 30 years earlier, it reached the height of its popularity in the 1950s. Almost every middle-class home in the United States and England had a television set. Every home, that is, except Agatha's. Agatha hated both radio and television. She believed that television would lead to the decline of the family. She also feared that television would replace books and prevent people from learning.

But television producers liked Agatha's books and knew how popular they were. They knew that television adaptations of these books would attract a huge audience. They chose her book *And Then There Were None* for this television debut. Agatha would have been appalled at the production. Everything that could have gone wrong did. The film setting had been changed to a hotel in the Austrian Alps in winter, instead of an island off the coast of Devon. The film was also poorly directed and produced on a very limited budget.

When Agatha and Max returned to Nimrud in 1951, Agatha was 61 years old. She had more difficulty getting around than when she was younger. But her good humor and bright spirit helped her deal with some of the difficult or uncomfortable times on the dig.

Desert weather was unpredictable. It was usually dry

and hot with a light breeze, but conditions could change rapidly. One year it rained constantly. Water dripped into Max and Agatha's house through numerous leaks in the walls and ceiling. The next year, however, hot dry winds accompanied by sandstorms prevailed throughout the digging season. Sand filled every corner of the house and covered every book, every paper.

Agatha accepted these uncomfortable conditions with calmness and serenity. She loved her time in the desert. Rain and sandstorms were infinitely preferable to five or six months of cold, damp English weather. Also, with few social commitments in the desert, Agatha could spend her free time planning and writing books.

Agatha and an assistant photograph archaeological finds at Nimrud.

Wherever she went, even in tiny countries in the Middle East, Agatha was recognized and followed. People begged her to autograph their books. Reporters requested interviews for newspapers and magazines. Visitors often pretended to visit the dig to learn more about archaeology. In reality, they wanted to get a glimpse of the famous novelist. They were usually disappointed. Agatha remained hidden in her writing room or in the building where most of the cataloguing and record keeping was done.

Agatha's fame grew with each book she sold. In 1951 the mystery magazine *Ellery Queen Digest* polled its readers, asking: "Who is your favorite mystery writer?" Agatha was voted one of the top ten mystery writers in the world. In 1961, when she was 71 years old, Agatha was the most widely read writer in the entire world. She had sold more books than anyone else in the world. Her books had been published in 102 countries. Several of them had been made into plays and full-length movies.

Agatha continued to be disappointed and frustrated with the way her books were rewritten for the stage. She didn't feel that they were adaptable for the theater. Agatha suggested to producers that they would be better served by writing a whole new story than by trying to make her books into something they were never meant to be.

In 1965 Agatha completed *Agatha Christie: An Autobiography.* She and Max spent the next few years traveling all over the world. She accompanied him to New York City, where he was to receive an award. Reluctantly, Agatha granted several interviews while in New York. She would only answer questions about her writing. If an interviewer began to ask personal questions, Agatha would quickly end the interview.

The fame that Agatha achieved through the years did not change her. She remained kind and generous to her family and friends. She would not allow talk about her writing to monopolize a conversation. She sometimes even had some difficulty in thinking about herself as a writer: "Never, when I was filling in a form and came to the line asking for occupation, would it have occurred to me to fill it in with anything but the time-honored: married woman. As a sideline, I wrote books. I never approached my writing by dubbing it with the grand name of 'career.'"

In 1971 Queen Elizabeth bestowed a special honor on Agatha by giving her the title of Dame Commander of the British Empire. After this, she was officially known as Dame Agatha Christie.

As she got older, Agatha became more reclusive. She spent most of her days at home in Greenway House. Her happiest times were visits with family and friends.

In 1975 Agatha's health began to deteriorate. Max and Rosalind spent much of their time looking after her. In October she had a heart attack that left her weak. Two months later, Agatha lost her balance and fell into a window, sustaining severe head injuries. In January 1976 Agatha caught a cold and never recovered. She died on January 12 at the age of 86. Her family, friends, and people all over the world mourned Agatha's passing.

Agatha Christie remains one of the most popular mystery writers in the world.

EPILOGUE

Agatha was buried on the grounds of a small church near her home. At the memorial service held for her a few months after her burial, Sir William Collins, Agatha's publisher for many years, spoke about her work. He said that Agatha "possessed in supreme measure one mark of literary greatness, the art of telling a story and holding a reader in its thrall, mesmerized by the narrative."

Agatha Christie wrote and published 67 mystery novels, 16 plays, 146 short stories, and 6 Mary Westmacott novels. Her mystery novels and short stories have been made into plays, movies, and television presentations. One of her plays, *The Mousetrap,* has been produced hundreds of times by theater companies in the United States and England. It has become one of the longest running plays in stage history.

Since 1975, six of Agatha's books have been made into full-length movies, including *Ten Little Indians, Death on the Nile,* and *The Mirror Crack'd.* In 1982, the BBC created a show called *The Agatha Christie Hour,* featuring several of Agatha's short stories. Between 1983 and 1989, eighteen of

Agatha's play The Mousetrap *has been running continuously in London for more than forty years.*

Agatha's novels were adapted for television. The Christie estate, however, closely guards Agatha's works. More than one director has approached with an offer to make a movie or television production, but permission is rarely granted. Agatha's family knows that Agatha was greatly disturbed and saddened by the recreations of her novels. "They gave me too many heartaches," she once said.

Agatha's autobiography was published after her death and was as popular as her murder mysteries. In it, Agatha expressed her gratitude for the quality of her life: "A child says, 'Thank God for my good dinner.' What can I say at the age of seventy-five? Thank God for my good life, and for all the love that has been given to me."

Sources

p.18   Janet Morgan, *Agatha Christie* (New York: Alfred A. Knopf, 1985), 34.

p.21   Agatha Christie, *Agatha Christie: An Autobiography* (New York: Berkley Books, 1977), 118.

p.26   Ibid., 93.

p.37   Christie, ...*Autobiography*, 242.

pp.37–38   Agatha Christie, *The Mysterious Affair at Styles* (New York: Bantam Books, 1983).

p.38   Christie, ...*Autobiography*, 245.

p.56   Charles Osborne, *The Life and Crimes of Agatha Christie* (New York: Bantam Books, 1984), 39.

p.59   Christie, ...*Autobiography*, 344.

pp.60–61   Ibid., 423.

p.62   Ibid., 423.

pp.65–66   Ibid., 352.

p.69   Ibid., 456.

p.79   Ibid., 48.

pp.80–81   Agatha Christie, *Come Tell Me How You Live* (New York: Bantam Books, 1955), 61.

p.81   Ibid., 62.

p.90   Christie, ...*Autobiography*, 476.

p.91   Ibid., 484.

p.91   Christie, *Come Tell...*, xiii.

p.94   Christie, ...*Autobiography*, 459.

p.96   Ibid., 208.

p.99   Ibid., xi.

p.100   Ibid., xi.

p.103   Ibid., 418.

p.105   Lynn Underwood, ed., *Agatha Christie: Official Centenary Celebration, 1890–1990.* (New York: Harper Paperbacks, 1990), 96.

p.106   Christie, ...*Autobiography*, 519.

Bibliography

Christie, Agatha. *Agatha Christie: An Autobiography.* New York: Berkley Books, 1977.

Christie, Agatha. *Cards on the Table.* New York: Putnam, 1968.

Christie, Agatha. *Come Tell Me How You Live.* New York: Bantam, 1955.

Christie, Agatha. *The Mysterious Affair at Styles.* New York: Bantam, 1983.

Gill, Gillian. *Agatha Christie: The Woman and Her Mysteries.* New York: The Free Press, 1990.

Morgan, Janet. *Agatha Christie.* New York: Alfred A. Knopf, 1985.

Osborne, Charles. *The Life and Crimes of Agatha Christie.* New York: Bantam Books, 1984.

Underwood, Lynn, ed. *Agatha Christie: Official Centenary Celebration, 1890–1990.* New York: Harper Paperbacks, 1990.

Wagoner, Mary S. *Agatha Christie.* Boston: Twayne Publishers, 1986.

Wynne, Nancy Blue. *An Agatha Christie Chronology.* New York: Ace Books, 1976.

Agatha Christie's Novels and Short Story Collections Featuring Hercule Poirot and Miss Jane Marple

Hercule Poirot

The Mysterious Affair at Styles (1920)
Murder on the Links (1923)
Poirot Investigates (Short stories, 1924)
The Murder of Roger Ackroyd (1926)
The Big Four (1927)
The Mystery of the Blue Train (1928)
Peril at End House (1932)
Thirteen at Dinner (1933)
Murder on the Orient Express (1934)
Three Act Tragedy (1935)
Death in the Clouds (1935)
The ABC Murders (1936)
Murder in Mesopotamia (1936)
Cards on the Table (1936)
Poirot Loses a Client (1937)
Death on the Nile (1937)
Dead Man's Mirror (Short stories and novellettes, 1937)
Appointment with Death (1938)
A Holiday for Murder (1938)
The Regatta Mystery and Other Stories (Short stories, 1939)

Sad Cypress (1940)
The Patriotic Murders (1940)
Evil Under the Sun (1941)
Murder in Retrospect (1943)
Murder After Hours (1946)
The Labors of Hercules (1947)
There Is a Tide (1948)
The Mousetrap and Other Stories (Short stories, 1950)
The Under Dog and Other Stories (Short stories, 1951)
Mrs. McGinty's Dead (1952)
Funerals Are Fatal (1953)
Hickory, Dickory, Death (1955)
Dead Man's Folly (1956)
Cat Among the Pigeons (1959)
The Adventure of the Christmas Pudding and a Selection of Entrees
    (Short stories, 1960)
Double Sin and Other Stories (Short stories, 1961)
The Clocks (1963)
Third Girl (1966)
Hallowe'en Party (1969)
Elephants Can Remember (1972)
Hercule Poirot's Early Cases (Short stories, 1974)
Curtain (1975)

Miss Jane Marple
The Murder at the Vicarage (1930)
The Tuesday Club Murders (Short stories, 1932)
The Regatta Mystery and Other Stories (Short stories, 1939)
The Body in the Library (1942)
The Moving Finger (1943)
The Mousetrap and Other Stories (1950)
A Murder Is Announced (1950)
Murder With Mirrors (1952)
A Pocket Full of Rye (1953)
What Mrs. McGillicuddy Saw! (1957)
The Adventure of the Christmas Pudding and a Selection of Entrees
    (Short stories, 1960)
The Mirror Crack'd (1962)
A Caribbean Mystery (1964)
At Bertram's Hotel (1965)
Nemesis (1971)
Sleeping Murder (1976)

Index

Mallowan, Max (2nd husband), 71–73, 87, 88, 90–91, 93, 98, 102, 103; as archaeologist, 70, 76–77, 79–85, 94–96, 99, 100–101

The Man in the Brown Suit, 49

Marple, Jane (character), 62, 63, 76, 88, 91

Miller, Agatha Mary Clarissa. *See* Christie, Agatha; Westmacott, Mary

Miller, Clara (mother), 8, 12, 18–20, 31, 32; health of, 30, 34, 51–52; as mother, 7, 9–10, 13–14, 21–23, 26, 29, 33

Miller, Frederick (father), 8–9, 10, 12, 14–15, 18, 19

Miller, Madge (sister), 10, 11, 12, 19, 26, 27, 37, 45, 47, 52

Miller, Monty (brother), 11, 19

The Mirror Crack'd, 105

The Mousetrap, 105, 106

movies, 39, 100, 105, 106

The Murder at the Vicarage, 62, 63

The Murder of Roger Ackroyd, 50

Murder in Mesopotamia, 82

Murder on the Links, 45

Murder on the Orient Express, 77

The Mysterious Affair at Styles, 38, 40, 43–44

The Mystery of the Blue Train, 59

Nimrud, Iraq, 96, 98, 99, 100–101

Nineveh, Iraq, 70, 76, 77

N or M?, 90

One, Two, Buckle My Shoe, 89

Orient Express, 64–66, 71, 76–77, 95. *See also Murder on the Orient Express*

Paris, France, 16, 18, 19–20, 21–22, 24

Pau, France, 17–18

Peril at End House, 75–76

Phillpotts, Eden, 29

plays, 69, 102, 105

Poirot, Hercule (character), 39, 45, 48, 59, 69, 75, 77, 79, 82, 84, 88; description of, 37–38; first case of, 38, 44; last case of, 91

Queen Mary of England, 94, 95

The Regatta Mystery, 88

reviews, 47, 50, 85

Royal Flying Corps, 32, 34–35

Sayers, Dorothy, 74–75

The Scoop, 75

Scotland Yard, 55–57

The Secret Adversary, 45, 47

The Seven Dials Mystery, 60, 61

The Silent Spring, 91

Sketch, 45, 48

Sleeping Murder, 90

"Snow upon the Desert," 29

Styles, 51

television, 100, 105–106

Tell Brak, Syria, 84–85

Ten Little Indians, 105

Three Act Tragedy, 79

Three Blind Mice, 94

Torquay, England, 7–15, 20–21, 22–24, 31–32

Ur, 67–68, 71, 74, 76

West Indies, 62, 64–65

Westmacott, Mary, 69, 77, 91, 97, 105

Winterbrook, 79

Woolley, Leonard and Katharine, 67–68, 71, 74, 76

world wars, 34–36, 41, 87–91

Photo Acknowledgments

The photographs are copyrighted to and have been reproduced with the permission of: The Illustrated London News Picture Library, pp. 1, 33, 48, 51, 54, 56, 57, 58, 60, 83; Camera Press London, pp. 2 (photograph by Angus McBean, by kind permission of the Agatha Christie Centenary), 104 (photograph by G. Argent); Mary Evans Picture Library, pp. 19, 25 (both), 30, 34, 75; Archive Photos, p. 20, 92 (Popperfoto); Hulton Getty Picture Collection, pp. 35, 89; UPI/Corbis-Bettmann, pp. 42, 66, 67, 95, 101; Photofest, pp. 39, 63, 106; Underwood & Underwood/Corbis-Bettmann, p. 47; Corbis-Bettmann, pp. 64, 70; UPI/Bettmann, pp. 68, 72, 78, 86, 98; British Tourist Authority, p. 73.

Page 44: From *The Mysterious Affair at Styles* (jacket cover) by Agatha Christie. Copyright 1978. Used by permission of Bantam Books, a division of Bantam Doubleday Dell Publishing Group, Inc.

Page 61: From *The Seven Dials Mystery* (jacket cover) by Agatha Christie. Copyright 1981. Used by permission of Bantam Books, a division of Bantam Doubleday Dell Publishing Group, Inc.

Front cover photograph: Camera Press (Bassano) London.